¿How the fuck do I forget you?

Wake up happy again

R. Romojaro

FOREWORD

This isn't just another book; I don't even think it *can* be considered a book as such.

It's not a book with a funny story that you can use to entertain yourself on the way to work when you're on the subway, with little dragons, castles and princesses.

In this "book," I'm going to be clear and direct so that it may be more enjoyable, useful and effective. Step by step, and from my experience, I want to transmit to you how to get out of this shitpuddle you've now gotten yourself into and help you to get your head around things, to understand what is happening to you and to make you trust me so that you may soon stop suffering.

As I have said, my intention is that you be happy again and only after that will we see if you get back with her or not, or what the problem is. But the only thing that matters here is *you* and managing to get you to wake up happy again.

I'm going to be very direct and concise. They will be key things for you to overcome it, as if they were the instructions for the DVD player, where they make it very clear where you have to press for it to record the film when you're not at home or where you program it to turn off in case you fall asleep.

This is going to be a conversation from me to you, like the one you could have with your best friend when you call him in a complete mess and you say to him, "Dude, I need you to come. I feel like shit; I'll explain in a bit."

In fact, this book, if it can even be called that, will only work on the basis of your suffering. If you're really having a hard time, you will feel identified and devour the pages seeing that you're the protagonist of all of this and that it goes with you. If, on the contrary, you're reading just for the sake of reading—out of curiosity—it will probably seem stupid to you, exactly as if you were reading your neighbor's DVD player manual, which isn't even the same brand as yours.

Or maybe it'll do you some good; maybe you'll read everything and tomorrow, if you find yourself in the situation of being screwed up over love, you'll remember all of this and you'll know how to get over it from the first minute.

You also have to know that none of this will work until you've decided to heal. Nothing that you read will do any good if you don't have a sincere and clear intention to be well again. Let me explain:

- If you still doubt whether to forgive that cheating.

- If you still think you're going to chuck your pride down the drain and you're going to get back with her again almost in secret, without your buddies finding out, because you'd be ashamed of yourself if they saw you swallow everything and get back with her after everything that's happened.

- If it turns out that she lacks respect for you, you've already forgiven her a thousand times before and, even though you don't feel loved, nor do you see a future with her, the lack of balls you have to change the situation will make you forgive her yet again and keep putting up with things just because you're a coward and you're afraid to be alone.

If any of these is your case, DO NOT READ ON. Close this, go to WhatsApp (which you have right next to you) and send her a message telling her that you're a piece of shit, that you don't love yourself, that the whole self-love thing doesn't even sound familiar to you and that even *you* don't respect yourself, but that despite everything you still hope *she* does.

Keep reading if, on the contrary, you have realized that there no longer is a future with her, that what you need is to feel good again and to go back to who you used to be when you met her, when you still used to wake up happy.

If you've decided that you're going to start using that schlong of a head to think for once and you're going to accept that the main thing is *you*, that you're going to recover, that you're going to get rid of that anguish from your head and that pain from your heart and that once you're okay and life is pretty again, you'll decide whether you're going to try to get back with her or go for another "her", or for another "him"… or if better off alone, then please keep reading.

This will be the beginning of a tunnel that you have to go through. You'll have to enter with my directions and you have to know that there will be some shittily painful moments. There will be moments in which you want to go back, moments in which you despair because you're doing everything perfectly, but you have a bad day again and don't feel that you're moving forward.

There will be times when we go halfway along and you don't see the way out and you'll have to go ahead as an act of faith, for the sake of not giving up. You'll have to have balls and a cool head, so be true to yourself in this moment and decide right up to every last consequence if you want to heal, away from her, or if you still have doubts.

If you're sure about continuing, go ahead. Let's move on.

And if you're not, it's better for you to close this like I said to you before, but keep it somewhere where you can find it to continue from here when you need it, because believe me… You'll need it.

You'll headbutt yourself trying the impossible until one day, sick and tired of screwing up and seeing that you don't get better, you'll be faced with the thought of "enough is enough." Then that day you'll look for this very point for us to go on, exactly where we left off.

Either way, I want you to know that I decided to write this book one day as I was saying goodbye to the last person with whom I have shared my life, sitting in a park, in the sun, in Madrid, after a few ciders. Seeing that I would have to go through the same thing again, I wanted to use the revival of all the past feelings of heartbreak to write this and help whoever goes through the same thing in future, putting together the book that I myself would have liked to read many years ago when all of this was just too much for me and I thought that I would die of sadness and anguish.

I am the happiest man in the world when friends, friends of friends, acquaintances or people who have bought the book let me know that they have left their suffering behind and have started to wake up happy again, wanting to conquer the world.

I want to dedicate it to the memory and families of Pablo Román and Juan Manuel Pérez, two angels who were taken too soon to a better place.

Written in 2016 – 2017, in a land lost in the north of Scotland.

Your girlfriend has left you. Or you've seen something on her cell phone and now it turns out that you don't know if you can trust her again. Or worse: she was with someone else…

Or who knows, perhaps it's *you* who doesn't know what he wants and you've decided to leave it with her and, now that some time has gone by, you miss her and it's *her* who doesn't want to hear from *you*.

Or it might be that you've screwed up on a drunken day out and you've done something that you shouldn't have. Now she's left you because she feels betrayed and you feel terrible.

Well, however it may be, the story is (and that's why you're reading this) that you're a mess, that you're sick and tired of being like that and that you want to be okay.

Right then, let's get started.

The first thing that you have to keep in mind is:

Don't think that your case is special and that you suffer more than anyone else. Don't tell me that it was only a year but that it was very intense and that's why it hurts more now… nor that you were the ideal couple. You weren't; that's why you're not together anymore.

What's happening to you has happened to the vast majority of people in this world. Even if you want to stop reading with what I'm going to tell you—because it will seem stupid to you—what is happening to you is the most normal and even necessary thing there is.

In life, we will have (and what's more is that we need) good and bad moments. I suppose yin and yang will sound familiar to you, just like going through Hell while you study to then have a good job and enjoy the money or working like a bastard all day long in something that you hate but that will then allow you to buy the motorbike and be the happiest guy alive when summer comes. Yes, summer, in which, after much suffering between dieting and sport, you will strut off your abs in front of a group of hot girls who are watching you at the pool.

As you can see in all these cases, there finally exists a benefit. Think about when you were a baby and ask your parents about the fits you used to have when your teeth were coming out. You won't even remember, but I'm sure you suffered much more than now, when your gums would break as your teeth came out, you would get a fever and you wouldn't stop crying.

At that moment if someone had said to you, "hang on, because this is going to do you some good," I'm sure you would have thought "what a dickhead", right? How the fuck could this do you any good?

Okay, now think about what your favorite food might be: Pizza? A hamburger? *I* don't know. A steak? Barbecue ribs? Now tell me this: how could you have those moments of complete happiness with your wine, beer or Coca-Cola on vacation, in front of the sea, eating that very same dish, but without teeth? You couldn't! No way! And that is why, if you hadn't gone through that tough period, today you would have to feed yourself on baby mush.

You may now be thinking that the baby mush has to do with the suffering that you have. Right, what's happening to you is a moment of change and inflection in your life and you will no longer be able to turn back. So if I were you, I'd turn my internet data off so that WhatsApp doesn't distract me and I would read carefully, trying to take in everything I can.

Before I start, I want to make something clear to you: I am no smarter than you, or even close to it. What makes me the one who is writing and you the one who is reading is that I have already gone through this, and more than once. That's why I have already understood the reason for every feeling and for every thought. I learned to identify it and to realize that each time was the same; they are the same processes.

It's as if love had only one way of acting, regardless of who we are or whoever we're in love with. What's happening to you is that you've reached a moment of learning. The cure for your suffering and to make all this anguish and sadness go by is to grow as a person. There are no other ways around it, whether you like it or not. You have no other option left but to learn from this experience and grow. You will have to renew yourself and be an improved version 2.0 of who you've been until today.

Nothing, and I repeat NOTHING, is going to change if you yourself don't change. Start by assimilating this.

What exactly has happened? Even if you don't believe it, it doesn't matter. It's not important.

- It's just that I don't know why, but everything has grown cold.

- It's just that it's no longer like it used to be.

- It's not because of you, it's because of me.

- You have everything I like, but... I have doubts.

- I think I'm with you just for comfort, without any chemistry.

- I'll never find anyone like you, but...

- You deserve more than I can give you.

- I know I'm screwing things up and I'm going to regret it, but...

- I love you, but in another way.

- I feel suffocated by my ___ (job, friends, family, studies...).

- I have a lot of problems now. Solution: You gone.

- You're the best person I've ever met, but...

- I love you with all my soul, but I need to be alone.

- I'm leaving you because I feel alone.

- Things have grown cold.

- I love you so much that what's best is for me to leave you.

- It hurts me to make this decision, but... I think our relationship has no future.

- I want us to remain friends.

- I want to have a life of freedom.

- You will always be the most attractive guy in the world, but...

- I will never forget you, but...

- Thank you for the smiles and the good times, but...

- In the future, who knows, but at this point in time...

- I need to be alone to feel free.

- There is nobody else.

- I don't feel like you're the man of my life.

- Right now, I can't. Maybe in a few years' time I'll call you.

- I'm doing it for your own good.

- I've gotten used to being without you.

- I know you're the man of my life, but...

- It's not you, it's me.

- Eht's naht you, eht's mee (in a Texan accent).

- I'll regret it, but...

- I need time to see if I miss you.

- It's no longer the same as before.

- It's the best for both of us.

- I am very young and want to live life. Perhaps in the future.

- Our chemistry is over.

- I want to be a nun and I'm going to enter a convent.

- You deserve to be given 120% and I can't.

- I deserve something better than you.

- I want to be alone. I promise there's no one else.

- I love you so much, but I need time for myself.

- I have to concentrate on my career/studies.

- I'm a mess and I need time.

- I need some time with us separated.

Here, before going on, I would like to go over the famous "I need some time":

When they ask us for time to think, it usually means that they have already thought. It means that they don't want to be with us, but they're cowards and they don't have the balls to take a risk and take a step forward.

If someone loves us, they have to love us to death, and if not, it's not good enough to be half-assed.

When someone asks us for some time, of course we have to give it to them without thinking about it… In fact, we should give all the time in the world; that is, they can go get fucked from that very moment onwards.

I can't even imagine the cruelty of someone who leaves another person in a rotten mess, waiting and impatient, knowing that they're having a hard time, during "an indefinite amount of time". This is someone who goes on with their happy life, coming in and going out, knowing that the other person is suffering as they wait, which puts them at ease to know, because if things don't go well, they have the other one there for sure.

To Hell with "some time". You never needed time to know if you loved her; you always loved her.

I'm going to tell you about a different sort of love, but it's still love at the end of the day: does your mother sometimes need to give herself some time from you to see if she loves you?

Another example that made me realize is that I love the *Atlético de Madrid* and I don't only love them when they win. When we lose the fucking final once again and we are ruined, I go to my wardrobe, I grab my t-shirt, I don't take it off for two days and I love them even more. In fact, the worse they go, the prouder I am and the less I think about leaving them. Not once in my life have I ever thought about becoming a *Celtic* or *Betis* fan to see how a couple of weeks go, with the thought that "if it isn't my thing, I'll just go back to the *Atlético*."

Well, with this it's the same thing.

Giving time is a total mistake. The moment in which they ask us for some time, everything is already lost and it will only serve to destroy our nerves and sink our self-esteem. This can only end badly. Love is the simplest and most basic feeling we have. It's total binary; it can be "I" or it can be "O" and there's nothing in between. Either you love or you don't love. Being "confused" is "O"— that is, NOT loving—but she may be comfortable because you keep her company. What it certainly is not is "I" (= loving).

Loving is like getting married; either you *are* married or you're *not* married, but you can't be "a little bit married."

As you've seen with this, or with the examples earlier, whatever the reason may be, the end is always the same and it's that she doesn't want to be with you anymore.

You have to understand that love is free. You can't, let alone must you, tie someone up. In fact, that's precisely what is beautiful about all of this:

That someone, of their own free will, decides to share their time, their happiness and their life with you.

If she has done so for some time, but no longer wants to, respect it and understand that it's better to let the other person go than to try to retain them making them feel sorry for you, with sadness or, worse even, with blackmail. Don't fall for the mistake of holding on to someone who no longer loves you, who prefers to do other things in their life before sharing their time with you. Just be a worthy person, love yourself, respect yourself as much as the next guy and let her go.

And if it's true that you love that person, as a final present give them the most beautiful thing that can be given in this life, which is freedom.

Give them the freedom to choose, the freedom to go in peace and the freedom to not feel bad by knowing that they are hurting you with your decision. Simply smile, wish them the best, hug them and let them go.

Do it with honor, hug them and leave with your head held high. Act like a man and don't make a scene. You'll be doing a favor to yourself: you'll be sending the other person, but above all yourself, the message "if you don't love me, I don't care, because I love myself" and this—loving yourself—will be very important in this process of recovering and also in your new life.

And never, ever drag yourself along. Even if the other person hesitates and leaves you doors open, even if they tell you that they're not sure.

If they love you, they will come to you on their own without the necessity of you calling them, begging them or even going and crying to them.

And if it turns out that they never come back to you, it will mean that they definitively didn't love you anymore and that they preferred to be in bed and in the arms of someone who wasn't you or in no arms nor in any bed. But what's for sure is that they don't want to be either in *your* arms or in *your* bed. Therefore, as much as you beg them, making them feel sorry for you, it isn't the way to get them back, because they simply couldn't give a damn about being with you.

So learn to love yourself and to have dignity. Nothing is more important than you; you must constantly remind yourself of this.

Don't beat yourself up all the time if your partner meets someone else and you find out that they are cheating on you or you catch them with the plans to do so. Or maybe they've told you that they need some time away from you and, stupid you, you've gone and given it to them and have then discovered that that "time" was to go and bang someone else and calmly see if they're okay with their new mister or if they miss you and decide to come back to you after pleasing their body.

It's not your fault. Don't feel like an idiot; you did what you thought was best and the least suffocating for them. If there were other people, you didn't live a lie, you really did love and the problem is theirs, as they're the one who did live a lie and what's more is that it was by choice.

It's not even worth working yourself into a bad mood over this, nor should you feel ridiculous or be ashamed about not having realized. Don't feel like a fool; nobody sees you like that, only you in this situation of confusion. From the outside you see someone good being treated unfairly by a she-son of a bitch. Think if this happened to a friend of yours; would you think he's an idiot and her very smart? Or would you think that he has nothing to be blamed for, while *she* is a cum-wiping slut, and go on to have it in for her? Well there you go.

And don't waste time on revenge either. You can be sure that life will pay lies with fatter lies, and betrayals with even more screwed-up betrayals. However unhappy she has made you with her lies will come back to her multiplied, because that is what she has sown.

And when that moment comes, your best revenge will be your smile in her face, as you see how time has put her in her place.

Be strong, be intelligent and wait for your moment. Don't despair and don't get pissed off, letting your mouth loose on her or looking for the way to do her harm. You will only show her that you still care about her and that's why you act like that; it will be worse for you.

At this point, I want to tell you an anecdote of mine recounted in first person which is 100% real:

I was in love/obsessed with a girl, so much so that I saw her as being spectacular. I often even felt inferior to her, which, by the way, they notice miles away and makes them lose all interest, but well that's another story.

Everything was perfect. I admired her, I thought she was the most gorgeous woman I could aspire to—one of those women that make people say "what a thumping great girl this bastard has"—and I used to feel small next to her.

Well, because of life being what it is, which sometimes entangles everything, she started getting down and dirty with coke at her waitressing job and that's where things started to get twisted. Everything started to go shit color (as usually happens with coke) and from then on, there was just fall after fall, suffering and suffering again.

The girl ended up hooked as Hell and her life turned into a cluster-fucking mess, where she was high all day and full of lies. She wouldn't eat, she would barely sleep and she would even drink the water from the puddles at work.

And as tends to happen with love/obsession, I continued to see her as an amazing girl and carried on completely blind with her, even thinking that she was too much of a stunner for me and that she would end up going off with someone else (one of those new friends from shooting up together). In other words, I lost all of my self-love.

Well, after many months of tears, arguments, promises that everything would change, lies, relapses, bluffs to leave her a thousand times and the whole process involved in leaving a fucking toxic relationship until it's over, there came the day that I decided to put my balls on the table, say "enough is enough" and send her to go and get screwed for good.

I did so, knowing that it would be difficult, that it would involve mourning and a really tough period of time for me, as is normal, and often feeling unable to give her up. But I decided that I was sick and tired of losing my life to someone like that and that I was willing to suffer whatever was necessary.

And man did I suffer... I almost died, I suffered like a bastard for years and, what's more, I continued to love her and I continued to think of her 24 hours a day. I spent years without seeing any way out, without seeing any progress and without ceasing to having a tough time.

I would wake up in a foul mood, sad and full of hatred, and go to bed the same way every night. But then I decided to do something to fill up my time and I signed up for the gym, but not for health or anything like that, but rather with the thought of seeing myself in the future with a damn hot bod and how that would screw her over.

I decided to grow up like a man while I lived away from her and had no news of her life, with the idea of one day rediscovering myself, getting cold revenge and making her regret not being with the fine specimen of man I was going to become.

So moved by that pain, I decided to make money, work harder, learn to invest my money, be better looking... I decided with a huge inner rage to get looking at the top of my game and to be an attractive guy, so that in the future, when the moment came, I could pick up all my pride and self-esteem from wherever the Hell I had left them and go back to the city where she was for her to see what she had missed out on (a rather idiotic thought in hindsight, although I know that in your situation it would sound like glory to do something like that). Well, in the end, that effort was useful for many other things in my life.

That idea motivated me for many months, perhaps years even. I kept dreaming about her and I kept being slightly afraid of the day I would see her, to see what I was going to feel at that moment.

The day came, two years later, when I went back there one summer. I was bronzed, looked absolutely striking and was at the time getting to know a new girl, who just so happens to be the one largely responsible for me writing this now, although I may just tell that story later on. What's important is that I didn't go with her, but went alone.

I no longer cared about meeting up with her—I couldn't care less—and I didn't look for her, but I ended up bumping into her:

She was a rotten mess, drugged up to her coke ears and the only thing that came out of her was nonsense. Then on top of that, she even let slip a question: whether I wanted to bang her.

I was serene, normal, well dressed, with a good old beer and with friends. And the thing is that I felt sorry for her. I didn't even feel like bragging or making myself out to be interesting so that she could see how much I had improved and how much she had lost. I didn't want to get cold revenge like I had planned so many times before. Now I think of that and I think I felt like it would be like abusing someone inferior; it would make me a real prick if I had taken advantage of that moment to hurt someone so weak.

I immediately thought about how on Earth I could have felt inferior to her in the past. Then simply, in a tone that was neither good nor bad, but with the tone of someone who gives zero fucks about all of that (because they are above it all), I said no.

I told her that I wasn't going to go with her, or to have sex, or anywhere, that I honestly didn't feel like seeing her ever again and that I wished her luck, which she was probably going to need.

I turned around, finished off my beer and walked away calmly, oddly calm, knowing that at that very moment I had finally closed that chapter of my life. I felt that it was finally closing 100% and that it was also how I wanted it to be, with me remaining way above her and in awe because in the end I didn't have to achieve it by being bad, but rather that I had improved so much that the situation and the feeling came on its own.

She was in such a bad way, a shit-spitting train wreck, while I was damn fine. I noticed it; she noticed it even more. Never did she ever try to contact me again, I suppose because of her own self-shame. Nor did I contact her.

As you can see, I didn't need revenge, I didn't need to talk shit about her to our acquaintances and I didn't have to spend a single ounce of energy on doing her harm. I just needed to turn myself around, love myself and realize how much I'm worth and as I struggled to be someone better, I let time put each of us in their place.

That's why my advice is for you to rebuild your life on your side and not to waste your life, your time or your energy on something that's not worth it, such as seeking to cause harm with revenge.

Well, having now finished the anecdote, I repeat that however it may be, leave her; let her go. She's no longer your problem and you have to know how to say goodbye, slam the door, reinvent yourself and conquer the world. It will happen with friends as well and with jobs that run out. It will happen cyclically and you will have to overcome it to be better. Do you see yourself with balls and the will to do it?

If the answer is NO, it's a good moment for you to close this.

I understand that you're probably full of jealousy and rage because you think that right now, she's probably screwing her new little pal, and oh so happily, while you're in the piss-flapping dumps, locked in at home and dying of grief. It's only normal for you to feel that way; you think of her as being so yours that it makes you boil to think that someone else could touch her.

But let's go back a little bit, just so you can see that you shouldn't feel like such a jizzstain, because you weren't one. It's that goddamn cloud of sadness, anger, grief and jealousy that is blinding you and won't let you think clearly. I'm going to explain it to you as best I can and with other words.

Let's use you as an example:

Imagine that one day you wake up and things are great with your girlfriend, you get along like a house on fire and you're finally going to go on that little trip soon that you're so excited about.

You wish each other a good morning with a kiss, or over WhatsApp, or however, and each of you goes off to your own things, you to your classes and her to hers.

In the afternoon you go to the library to study because you feel calmer than at home, where there's always a lot of commotion, and while there concentrated on your own business, there suddenly appears a girl you have never seen there before. She has a beautiful little face and her smile when saying goodbye to her friend has caught your attention. You think "holy beJesus is this girl hot."

She comes in, she takes off her coat and it's not that she has a *pretty* face, it's that she's absolutely smoking.

Without further ado, she sits down, takes out her books and gets on with her own business. The afternoon goes by and you, after running your eyes over her a good number of times, finish doing what you have to, pick up your belongings and go home. And just like that, you forget about her. What the Hell were you going to do otherwise? Introduce yourself and treat her to a Fanta? And especially when you have your girlfriend at home, who you love so much. At the very most, you send a WhatsApp to the group you have with your pals and you tell them that one of them should come with you tomorrow to hit on her.

You come home and she asks you how your day has been. What do you do? Do you tell her that you don't know if you have been reading mathematics or English because with Angelina Jolie there in her prime you haven't taken in a thing? Obviously not; no way. You tell her it has gone well… that it was normal, that it was a bit of a drag, that you're tired, that you desperately want to finish the exams soon and that you love her a lot.

The truth is that you don't even think about the other girl. It was a good-looking girl and that's it, like thousands of them are. No way would you ever swap her for your girlfriend.

And then it turns out that the next day, as always in exam time, you go to the library to study in the afternoon and to have some peace and quiet there. And then she arrives. Today she's even better: she's wearing clothes that make the hot bod she has stand out even more and, on top of that, she's gorgeously dressed up. She's exactly the way you like girls to be: she's stunning, but she doesn't go around with too much make-up on, she straightens her hair just the way you like it and she knows how to dress. On top of all of this, you can see from her body language that she's very feminine.

She catches your attention again, and she awakens your instinct, but you keep going with your books. She walks over and sits near you, she smiles at you with that little face and she waves before sitting down and getting on with her own things. She's just such an angel. Oh, screw me.

You leave an hour later, sick and tired of not being able to concentrate because of how good she smells and thinking over and over about what she might be studying, where she might be from and what she has been doing around there recently when she had never been there before. You arrive home and once again the question: How has your day been? Good, like always...

And when you go to the library the following week, there she is. She greets you with a huge smile and you ask her how she is. She says well, you both talk a little and you take the opportunity to ask her all those questions that were pestering you: What she's doing there, what she studies etc.

She's lovely, she's very friendly and she seems at ease talking to you. You sit a bit away from her to study with a strange feeling, thinking that you like that girl.

You say goodbye to each other, talking a bit more, and you tell each other your names.

The next day you talk more, the next day more and even the day that she doesn't appear, without realizing it, you're hoping for her to come in through the door at any moment, looking for her with your eyes.

You definitely like this girl, or fuck that, you love her. And your girlfriend is still your girlfriend and she's the best… but freaking Hell do you like this other one. Do you think the time will come when you will come home and you will tell your girlfriend that an absolutely smoking girl comes to the library and that you like her more and more every day? What for? She's only an acquaintance from the library and the day might come when you don't see her anymore. You're not going to leave your partner for a girl you know from four afternoons there.

So anyway, the day comes when you go out with your friends and your girlfriend stays at home because her head hurts. You go out to have a couple of beers that end up being six, three rum and lemons and a shot of God-knows-what. Then you bump into this girl, who is also out with friends. As soon as you see each other, you run off to greet each other and you give each other a kiss on the cheek with a lot of love: too much love.

The truth is that you really are glad to see her, you love that feeling... and feck is she gorgeous.

Not a lot more happens. You fool around a bit, you shoot each other smiles—the occasional loving gesture— and you hold hands... You start to think that she likes you too.

Do you think it's finally time to tell your girlfriend what you feel for that stranger from the library, to tell her that you have bumped into each other today and that you spent the entire time together, but that you know little more than her name? I don't think you would.

At the end, the laughter comes out, the talking... you get to the point of looking for her on Facebook, the point of the WhatsApps arriving, the point of you not wanting to sleep with your girlfriend like you used to and the point of the mess in your head. Fuck, your girlfriend hasn't done anything wrong, but you can't avoid what the other one makes you feel and, obviously, you never stopped it because you never saw it as being anything dangerous.

She was just a girl who went to the library and you already had a partner. You didn't know when to cut the story, because you were sure of what you felt for your girlfriend. But little by little, you started to become confused. Being inevitable, the day will come when, if you're a man, before doing anything and being full of lies and tales, you will talk about it with your girlfriend and tell her the truth. You will break up, because you no longer feel the same way about her, but rather you now want to share your life with this new girl. You might even tell her through tears, because it breaks your heart to know that you're doing her harm when she doesn't deserve it. She's a wonderful woman and you have no doubt about it. But dammit, you don't love her and you can't do anything about it. It's not something you choose. If only we could consciously fall in love.

Or maybe you're the complete opposite of what a man should be and you're full of lies and bullshit until she catches you. The truth always comes out and everything ends much worse; you do much more harm to the person who has loved you so much for all this time.

Be that as it may, what choice did you have in all of this? You had to follow what you felt and you saw no more future with your ex-girlfriend. Your desire and joy were in this new girl and you didn't treat your ex like an idiot. You never said anything about what was happening, because there was nothing to worry about and when there was, it was already too late.

You would have acted like this, right? And what if we now used your ex as the protagonist of this story and you as the one who stays at home because your head hurts? Is it understandable?

It may be that your rage and jealousy are screwing you alive, but it all comes back to the same thing. It's not that she's humiliated you or that you're been an asswipe for not having seen it coming; it's simply that she doesn't love you anymore.

A separate case is the person who is with you and has been bumping off everything that has been put on them by way of immaturity, lack of self-esteem or simple hoeing around. However it may be, in this latter case, she didn't love you then, nor does she love you now, nor will she ever love you. If that is what has happened, you should be in eternal gratitude to life for having gotten rid of such a being for you.

The conclusion of all of this is that for two people to be together, you need love. You need for them to love each other, nothing else. If two people don't carry on together, it's because at least one of them no longer loves the other. If you live in Madrid and the other person in Tokyo and both of you love each other, you will do the impossible to be together. You won't stop thinking about her and she won't stop thinking about you and the excuse of the other person being far away won't work. You will both wait however long is necessary and you will make every decision in your lives consciously or unconsciously to bring you closer and closer to each other and finally be together. I suppose it's that famous "fuerza del corazón" (strength of the heart) that Alejandro Sanz used to sing about in Spanish.

So I hope you have understood and internalized this:

Respect the other person's decision and let them go. If you really do love her as much as you say you do, give her freedom, which is the most beautiful thing there is in this life. Hold your head high and love yourself. The sooner you assimilate these basic things, the sooner you will get out of this.

Quote from Fmaster in 2011:

She's not like ALL GIRLS; she's like we ALL are. We seek our happiness. As a general rule, leaving us is not an act of evil. They have simply stopped loving us and they leave us. They are in their perfect right as much as it upsets us. Then there are also many ways of doing this. They are all going to hurt. If they do it right, it will hurt us less than if they do it wrong. But whether we have a bad or worse time depends largely on ourselves. A lot of the time, expressions come out like "why is she doing this to me now?" Wrong point of view. They are not doing something to you that hurts for that purpose. They have their interests in mind and while they may do something that hurts us, it will be out of selfishness and not out of evil.

DO NOT DESPAIR

Never, ever despair in bad times. Everything negative has an end and everything positive too.

You could be the happiest person in the world and there will come a point in time when the happiness ends because something bad will come. The good thing about this is that it will also happen the other way around, so do not despair over it and make sure it's clear to you that all of this will pass by and you will be happy again. Once more you will have tough times in the future and you have to understand all of this as part of life, realize how beautiful it is, love it as it comes and take this as part of the learning you have to do.

Even if you see things as being quite grim now, even if you are having a tough time now and even if you don't see a way out, everything is shit or you even think that the world is ending on you, DO NOT DESPAIR. Just make sure this is clear and have faith. I promise you this: that THIS IS GOING TO BE OVER AND YOU ARE GOING TO BE HAPPY.

DO NOT DESPAIR. While that day comes in which you wake up happy, which *will* come, simply try to make the road as smooth and bearable as possible. And with all of this, you will make yourself stronger, wiser and more of a man.

Imagine that life is a mountain hike with ups and downs and you have a sled, which are your experiences, and they go with you.

You've been sliding, enjoying yourself down the mountain, having a good time and laughing. You've reached the bottom, where you are right now, and now it's time for you to grab the sled and drag it to the top again, struggling and suffering. When you have arrived, you will be someone else because of having carried the weight of the sled during the entire climb. On top of this, you will also know how to better appreciate every second of the next descent sliding down, knowing how difficult it is to return to the to. When you get to the bottom, you will have to grab your sled and climb an even bigger mountain again, you will have to get to the top even stronger and you will do so with the motivation of someone who knows that at the end of the path of suffering and pulling the sled along, there is a huge reward waiting for you.

Life is bringing you something positive, something you cannot even imagine. DO NOT DESPAIR and have faith that at the end of the path you have your reward. Look at it this way: even light begins to beam out for just an instant after the maximum darkness of every night.

Have faith that you will wake up and live happily again. Nobody dies from this and you have to do things pretty badly to end up creating a trauma for yourself.

I quote what El Crápula wrote in 2008 to illustrate all of this:

Facing pain is good; it makes you be reborn. What is bad is getting closer to the source of pain. From these bad moments, a strong person learns a lot. Ask yourself the following question and record it in your head. Why does she deserve, after treating you as she has, for you to shed tears on her behalf? Are you really willing to lose your battle against yourself, for someone who has shown they don't love you? You will soon be far above that.

You only have two options:
Not to get her back and not to recover, or not to get her back and recover. Everything that comes out of there is like trying to change the moon's orbit. You can't. She didn't escape from you; she left, because she wanted to and once she did this, you can do nothing to make her come back, but you can do a lot for yourself. Keep your spirits up,

SELF-LOVE AS A CURE

Love yourself. Love yourself more than ever. Use that rage, that desire for revenge, that sadness, all that in your favor and make them useful to get out of this instead of being what you are worst at managing in this moment of your life. Be intelligent. I am going to give you different examples so that in this way you can understand it more easily:

There are people with broken hearts who feel that they don't want to be in the same city as the other person and decide that it's time to fly, to take the suitcase and to go to that city overseas where they always imagined making new friends, learning a language and starting a new life: something that always excited them but that they never had the balls to do.

Others take refuge in sports. They decide to finally get rid of that beer gut, to wax themselves up, to buy themselves expensive clothing that they wouldn't have even thought of buying before (because "what for, if I already have a girlfriend or barely even go out…?") and to be a good-looking guy: something they didn't used to do because of laziness, because if they were going to do sport they didn't have time for their girlfriends or whatever other excuse.

And now they decide to look after their diet. They leave bad habits like tobacco, alcohol or getting high up to the sky every weekend.

They eat healthily, they do a lot of sport, which makes them feel good, they try doing weights, boxing, football, swimming—whatever—they make new friends, they meet healthier people and they fill their heads with other motivations while they become people with more and more light every day, with a better appearance and who women begin to like, ceasing to be someone gray and run-of-the-mill and ceasing to transmit sloppiness, to now attract attention.

There is also another kind of people that I have met and who basically out of rage—the type that would be provoked by the thought that she left with another guy or that she had left them now completely indifferently with so many plans in the way—have concentrated on finishing their studies with an awesome mark and have managed to find a freaking amazing job, always thinking of being able, when time went by, to make their ex screw themselves over on the inside upon seeing that they were now a winner in life, with a good car and new apartment while she was still at that shitty job, imagining the moment in which she realized just how much she had lost and she tortured herself thinking about how she had screwed up and how much of a dickpole she was for not noticing that fine example of a man she'd had.

If you notice in all these examples, the person who was down in the dumps has proposed himself to grow some balls, grow up and stop being the redneck hillbilly who had never left his neighborhood, to stop being the flabby man who was embarrassed to take off his shirt at the pool or to stop being so sad, in order to be a person with a good job with enough money to spare to be able to bury his ex in bank bills.

This example of a person who decides to redirect their feelings to create something productive is what you should do to get out of this one. Grow, don't stop, don't settle for less and strive. It will cost you work and you have to do your part, so set yourself a goal and go for it. The path to achieving it will make your head be distracted and have less time to suffer and reaching your goal will make you feel proud of yourself and be an improved version of yourself. Be whatever your goal may be, set it for yourself and go for it. This is essential.

In addition, having new motivations will make your head take seconds away from the constant suffering due to the emptiness you have for your ex in order to dedicate them to new goals.

You also have to take into account that there is the opposite side, which has touched me closely: friends of mine who got up half crying, with comments like: "Oh, everything is so shit… I've dreamed of her again…," "well, I'm going to see if I can arrange to speak to her," "I'm going to go to my mother's house to see if she regrets things with time and she calls me when she feels alone" etc. This is like banging your head against the wall over and over again and getting up and hitting the same wall time and time again, before waking up in a pretty screwed-up state and sad and hitting the wall again and so on in a cycle that will repeat itself until you open your eyes.

You can do it if you want to, as many times as you want, but I promise that in the end you will have to take the first example to be followed. You will have wasted precious time being fucked-up too, which, if you had used it properly, would now possibly have allowed you to be recovered and the happy person you were some months back.

If you are determined to choose the first example, keep reading. I will explain how to get out of this and be three times stronger in the face of life for whatever comes later on.

I bet you're now dreading getting on Tinder and finding her, huh?

Come on, let's talk seriously:

You're probably scared to be at home, in your room, or simply alone. The thoughts get into your head and make you suffer and you're afraid to go through that area where you might bump into her. You may even see her with another guy; you panic just thinking about it.

Everything reminds you of her and distresses you and you are sick and tired of not being able to get her out of your head all day. As soon as you wake up, you will probably have a feeling of relief because in dreams you have stopped thinking about her, but then straight away—the second you open your eyes—the thoughts return like a black cloud that doesn't let you think.

You are clumsy, joyless and you just can't. You let the days go by suffering and you don't see a way out of this. You don't know what the feck to do and, what is worse, from time to time you see a photo of hers on Facebook and... Oh McJesus freaking Hell!! She's happy!! She's with her friends, going out, going on trips, having fun, laughing...

And you? You down in the dumps... down and without relief. There is no band-aid, no aspirin and nothing that they can tell you to relieve you.

You get yourself unconscious until you come home on all fours and drunk there. You don't care about anything and that partly alleviates your suffering. But the hangover multiplies the anguish of the following days by ten, so I don't think the solution involves alcohol.

Okay, now that you must have just thought "fuck, this guy knows exactly what I'm going through," let me help you get out of this one.

LOVE OTHERS, BUT YOURSELF THE MOST

You have to love yourself. You have to know how much you are worth and you have to stop feeling empty without her. You were born alone and you will die alone, just like we all will. You cannot depend on someone you found on the street; you don't need absolutely anyone, other than yourself, to move on in every situation.

Love yourself

Learn to love yourself. Learn that it's necessary in order to love others, and for them to love you, that you first love yourself. You have to respect yourself. And for fuck's sake, don't self-humiliate yourself. Show everyone, and yourself first, that you are above it all; you have to have pride and self-love. Do not drag yourself along. If she doesn't love you, it's over. She has to leave. You don't care, because your life is freaking amazing. You don't need anyone and if she wants to share her life with you, then great. But if not, she's the one who loses.

Do not make a scene

Don't muck around, don't go over to her house with a bouquet of flowers while it's raining, thinking that that will soften her heart and that she will come out running to give you a hug, because that only happens in movies. While in your head she will realize that you are both one for the other and everything will be resolved, what has a greater probability of happening is that she's there with her new mister and looks out the window and says "oh God, this drag of a guy is here again" and they both laugh their dicks off at you.

Create the version 2.0

Grow and become stronger, more handsome, more intelligent, more educated and more interesting.

Nothing can stop you

Start to see all the good things that you have inside and realize the enormous power that you have. There is nothing impossible; you can achieve absolutely everything.

Love yourself. No matter what you're like, you're unique among the eight billion people there are on planet Earth.

You don't need to be bitter about something like that. Keep a cool head and make decisions out of honor and intelligence. When all of this is over, you will thank yourself for not having lost your pride dragging yourself along, begging or even crying.

START FEELING GOOD

Let's be clear. There are two ways to get out of this:

• One is long and fucked up.

• The other one is super long and super fucked up.

If you have chosen the second option, continue as you have until now. Keep yourself locked up at home thinking about her, keep stalking her social network pages or keep calling her without really knowing what for.

You will be a pain in the ass, you will beg, you will create a bad vibe that will leave you even more screwed up and you will end up suffocating her.

In the end you will end up seeing her with someone else, because she will be more intelligent than you and will rebuild her life. Perhaps you even put your foot in it and say or do something you shouldn't out of spite and her new boyfriend ends up smashing your face in.

If this happens, over time, a long time, you will come to accept that there's nothing that can be done and you will give up. Over the years, you will lose all hope between hatred and resentment, keeping all of this shit inside you.

I wish you luck if that is the path you choose and I'll be here for when you want to resume your recovery in the only possible way.

If you choose the first option, let's go with a clear and concise rule:

CUT OFF ALL CONTACT AND START DOING SPORT.

It's essential that you cut off absolutely all contact with that person, even with friends in common who could talk to you about her.

There are no exceptions. You will not hear about her again from friends, nor from family members, nor will you look at her social network pages, nor her WhatsApp photo or anything, absolutely anything.

Now perhaps you are making the excuse that, since are you going to cut off the relationship with her friend Susan or Mary or I don't know, you get along really well with her and, in addition, she has your Lord of the Rings trilogy.

Well yes, it doesn't matter what excuse comes to mind. Cut off any relation to her; there is no other solution. You can buy it again and she can keep the other one. Frodo can go and take a pole up his ass.

If it turns out that you were boyfriend and girlfriend and cousins all at the same time (like pretty much every Royal Family in Europe) and you have family in common and are going to see each other at Christmas lunch... Well, obviously you're not going to go and hide in a bunker or go with earplugs in your ears.

In that situation, be cordial—"hello" and "goodbye"—without entering into further conversation. And if someone wants to talk to you about her, you cut them off and say you don't want to know anything about her.

In addition to doing you good to be able to recover, it will make you look like a guy who is elegant and has some balls.

Imagine the opposite case: the image you would give off if you were like a little whining boy moping around in the corner and speaking badly about her out of resentment. How embarrassing if that were to happen.

Use the family example for friends if you are/were from the same group.

But still, avoid everything without exception. It's very important to do it for a good period of time in order to recover. And if you have to find new friends, you can look for them.

Everything will be easier if, instead of doing it because a certain Romojaro tells you to, I explain why. So here I go:

It's a chemical withdrawal syndrome of the brain, which you arrive at from an emotional dependence on the other person.

The brain secretes chemical substances depending on the moment. Be aware of the following: you can feel the adrenaline when something scares you and you have to run away or you can notice the endorphins that make you feel good after beating yourself up and sweating doing sport, just like you can also see the sadness you have when hungover until the brain readjusts the serotonin levels.

Right now, your brain is in shock, deregulated by what it's gone through and that's why you have moments of extreme anguish in which you want to travel the world until you reach her door. Then when you're there, you talk, you give each other a hug and the brain secretes chemical substances that make you feel good. You say goodbye (again) forever and on the way home you are happy and calm. You think it's over and now you really do feel strong… but a day goes by and the brain goes back to having "cold turkey" withdrawal symptoms of that substance that was secreted upon being with her and starts despairing again.

Maybe you're drunk in the bathroom of some bar and while you pee with your vision blurred from how blindly wasted you are, you realize that you couldn't give two flying fucks about her and everything can all go to Hell. And the next day, all hungover, you can't get her out of your head and you just want to cry. Maybe you're not at all hungry and you can't eat anything, you're freezing cold in July and you're not sleeping at night, nor do you need to. But then your cell phone rings and you think it's her. You race to take it out and... It is! You speak to her for a minute, you hang up and now you're finally hungry, warm and sleepy. This all goes back to the same thing: a chemical withdrawal syndrome of the brain. (Yes, it's sad, but love is a mix of chemical reactions in our heads).

I even remember having quite absurd thoughts, which I later realized were recurring in others too, such as wishing for a misfortune to happen so that we would have to see each other again. Or I used to be sure that, if they offered me the chance to win the lottery or get back together with her, I would choose her without hesitating.

Also, it stands to reason that your brain fools you: you only remember the good and you see everything dark without her. Obviously, as is only normal, the brain wants its chemical fix and will fool you for it. It will tell you that it doesn't matter if you speak or if you see her Facebook and it will paint your future black if it's not with her etc. It's even the most normal thing ever that in the final flicks of your dependency you dream of her; these are symptoms of the brain no longer knowing what to do for you to give it what it wants and starting to give up.

You may have noticed that it's like a drug. After the shot, or the fix or whatever, you feel good and calm, you even see things positively and you can handle everything. But when a few hours go by, or perhaps days, the brain demands its dose again and if you don't give it to it, it goes back into its depressed state: you relapse into apathy and sadness, thinking about it until you collapse and suffer again.

And it would be relieved momentarily with another dose, talking to her again, for example, restarting the process in a continuous cycle.

It's obvious that some sort of chemical process in our brain simulates that withdrawal syndrome that the drug has and that's why your brain will deceive you. It will make you think "call her; there's nothing bad in doing so." It will stick this in your head so that you contact her and you give it its fix, in any way possible.

Even when you're strong and don't do it for weeks, your brain will play new tricks to achieve it and calm its addiction: it will make you dream about her.

This is part of the process; it's inevitable.

Right, I don't know if there might be some sort of drug addiction that can be cured by sticking more of it in your body when it asks you for it, but I don't think there is. And in this case in particular, I assure you that there isn't.

The way to heal from the addiction is to distance yourself from her, nip it in the bud, suffer the necessary until your body and your mind realize that they don't need it to live or be happy.

The only way you can get over the void of her absence is to get used to that absence.

Once I was out with a friend of mine to buy something to eat and she was telling me how sad she was because her boyfriend had slept with a lot of girls while they were going out. She caught him because she installed I-don't-know-what in his cell phone without him realizing and she monitored him by GPS from another country. Imagine how pissed off she was.

It turned out that he would go at night to a mountain there was in their city where couples go to get done what needs to be done and he was there for two hours and then went home.

When she asked him what he had done during the day, he said that he was at a friend's house, playing a few FIFA games.

As we were entering the Chinese minimarket to buy some macaroni, I asked her "Do you want to get cured? Well from now on, you have to care as much about him as you do about the Chinese lady who's putting the macaroni in the plastic bag. Do you care what the Chinese lady does or says? Do you look for her on Facebook? Do you ask for her number to see her WhatsApp photo and see who she goes out with? Well the same thing with your ex." At that moment she found it funny. She realized with time that I was right.

Well the same with you: keep away from her. Your life is now going the other way. Don't look for her, don't ask about her, nothing. That person doesn't exist to you. This is literal. She isn't that loving and sincere person who loved you and made you happy. Now she's someone with the same ass or the same smile, but not the person you fell in love with.

Let time go by. There are no exceptions. Every time you act like that, you will be getting out of this addiction. Every time you break the zero-contact rule, you will fall again and you will have to start all over again from the beginning. Do not despair if this happens; we normally all screw it up a few times until we're sick and tired of seeing that we fall and that no progress is made. We realize that we've lost precious time and then, upon seeing that there is no other path, we start to really apply the zero-contact rule.

I would like to be able to tell you that there are exceptions to this zero-contact rule, that there is a way in which you talk to her and continue to see her or hear from her and that it will not hurt... But the truth is that there isn't. I assure you that if you listen to me and cut off all contact every day, you will be slightly better off and I also assure you that, if you do not, you will not get better, which is what we are here for, right?

You have to know that it's now all going to feel like a kick to your heart and another to your balls. If you see on Facebook that she's going to the shopping mall with her friend, your thought will be that she's going to go and buy herself some sexy clothes to go out this weekend = suffer. If she appears in a photo alone in the middle of the countryside, you'll think that she's gone with some guy who's banging her = suffer. If she appears buying herself a phone, you'll think she's going to change numbers to have a thousand guys on WhatsApp from every weekend out without you seeing her connection time = suffer. And so on and so forth: it's all going to be paranoia and bitterness from your state of heartbreak, so start this very day to delete her from your social network pages, delete her number from your cell phone—even though you know it by memory, it doesn't matter—delete the chat from WhatsApp, get rid of her photos from your room: everything, absolutely everything gone, as if she didn't exist.

It will only be momentary, so don't worry. It will last the time that you need to be okay again and afterwards, you will be able to resume all contact again, when the pain doesn't anguish you and when you wake up happy again with a clear head.

Avoid the low moments, those when you despair and want to call her, when the withdrawal symptoms from her make you send her a WhatsApp or go to pick her up from work. When you feel like that—when you despair—call your best friend, go outside or put your sneakers on and go for a run, whatever, but don't spend any more time doing what you're doing while your thoughts beat you up until torturing you.

You will have low moments where your very brain fools you with an "it doesn't matter if you call her" or "send her a WhatsApp and tell her that you're outside her house, because that's exactly what she wants" so that you give it its next fix. Avoid it, be strong and do it for yourself. Get out of wherever you are, leave what you're doing and start doing something different, whatever. If it's something physical that includes you sweating and tiring yourself out, it will help a lot more than getting on the PlayStation or X-videos, for example.

Managing to endure the lows is the hardest part of this whole process. If you have enough balls to know that you have to get through that moment and move on, you will have more than half the road behind you and with each low point that you resist, you'll be giving another blow to the "cold turkey" withdrawal feeling from her and you'll have killed her just that little bit more.

Plus, think about it properly: How could crying over the phone or sending a ridiculous love/spite SMS at 5:00 in the morning help you? Seen from the outside, you would only make a fool of yourself.

There's something important I want to tell you with an example so that you properly understand and internalize all of this: you have a broken heart; it's shattered and run down like shit.

The heart is what we have to feel. Sometimes, it will even literally hurt in the middle of a low moment when it feels like you're dying of grief.

Your head is okay, supposedly. We use our heads to think and to make decisions.

We can't feel with our heads. You can't say "I'm going to fall in love with this girl, because it'll be good for me, because her parents have money," for example.

We can't think with our hearts either. This means that if your heart makes you make the decision to desperately call her in the middle of the night (in tears)... Don't do it. Bad decision. You will drag yourself along and you will make her feel sorry for you. But pity and falling in love are not compatible. You fall in love with someone you admire, not someone who makes you feel sorry for them. Not even in movies have I seen a hot secretary from

New York fall in love with a poor man who sleeps in front of an ATM.

If your heart asks you to go to her workplace to speak with her, if your heart asks you to send her flowers, if your heart blah blah blah, DON'T FUCKING LISTEN. Your heart is made to feel and your head to decide and you're going to be able to decide even less with your heart, given how it is right now. If you're thirsty, would you really grab a glass from the table with your foot instead of with your hand? And even less so if you have your foot in a cast, right?

Now is the time for your head to take control and know how to get you out of this mess. May your heart remain calm, may it rest, may it recover, may it take a vacation to be perfect again and may it go at its own rhythm and come back at 200%, because, even though it sounds like gobbledygook, believe me: you will need it to be able to love again further on.

Remember, don't mess it up and don't put your foot in it when you're on a low.

When you are distressed and when your head is making you suffer, tough luck and put up with it.

Those moments happen. They might be minutes. Completely change the situation, start doing something else and when you're calm, when you can think clearly, *then* you can decide if you want to break the zero-contact rule or if you want to keep fighting a little more for yourself and for your happiness.

100% of the times you desperately break the zero-contact rule, you will be thrown down into the emotional dumps, where you will have to suffer three times as much to be able to get back to the point before everything went tits up. I give you my word on that. And so that you see that I'm not lying about anything, if you do that, you will suffer and you will remember this sentence and think "he was so right."

It goes without saying that a "let's arrange to meet and talk" or "let's have dinner and say goodbye to each other and do things properly" or something which scandalizes me—meeting up to have three beers and ending up in the same bed—is the worst thing you can possibly do.

None of this is going to make her, even though she's told you that she no longer wants to continue with you, decide that she now does. And the only usefulness that it will have will be to raise her ego in the same proportion in which yours falls.

She will leave happy and calm, knowing as my father says that "when they go 'pss', you wag your tail" and that you are still there like a little lapdog. As for you, you will sink in shit until your ears when she still doesn't want to hear from you, which will be even worse for you because of having seen her so recently.

The answer to any of these things should come from you. Think for a moment: Do you want to be half-with her? Do you want her to meet up with you like she does with another 20 guys? Or is it that, on the contrary, you deserve someone who loves you? If you settle with being just another guy in her life, it means that you haven't learned anything until now: you don't love yourself for shit and you can't wait for her to do so. Do you not realize that?

I understand that there are times when you have to talk, that she still has some of your things, that you both have to work out what to do with the vacation reservations that you've made etc.

Very well then, apply the rule of the Chinese lady who sells you the macaroni. Do you give *her* explanations of what you're going to do with the money? Do you ask *her* if she's hooked up with anyone? Or do you simply say "hi," do what you have to do, say "thank you" and leave?

Here it will be her ego that falls, while yours rises.

You may even think now that you're going to look like a weirdo. Well, this is the attitude that is best for you for your heart to recover, neither more nor less, and you don't care about what she thinks about you or the way you act, just like you don't care what the Chinese lady thinks about the tattoo you've gone and gotten or the car that you want to buy.

And now one thing between you and me: if there used to be the slightest chance that she would come back to you, it's acting like this that she realizes how you love yourself, that you value yourself, that it's her ego that falls and her who notices the void that hopelessly losing you causes. If that were to happen, I can tell you right now that sequels were never good, without any exception. But oh well; you can decide there. I'll go through it all in detail in the following chapter.

Are you determined to cut off all contact? If the answer is "no," close the book and do me a favor: give it to someone with balls who really does want to get out of this and not to a pussyflap like you.

If the answer is "yes," let's move on to what comes next.

I'm including a quote here from Erreaxe in 2012, which exemplifies all of this quite well:

When someone who, despite loving you, leaves you and they realize they've made such a big mistake, they don't go looking for you, saying things for you to feel pity for them.

They go looking for you to beg your forgiveness and an opportunity, to recognize their mistake and tell you that they love you and, if it's necessary, they self-flog themselves.

When someone who doesn't love you leaves you and realizes that they miss the comfortable life they had with you, they will look for you saying things for you to feel pity for them.

Things like: "I'm having a terrible time," "I don't sleep at night," "I miss you," "I need you in MY life" and "come and get back with me."

"Come and get back with me"? WTF! You left me and you want ME to come back, as if, on top of everything, you were doing me a favor.

When someone loves you, they don't ask you for an "even if we just talk occasionally," THEY ASK YOU FOR A FUCKING OPPORTUNITY for you to let them back into your life.

A couple is an "US" not a "ME," "ME," "ME." The words "come and get back with me" mean exactly that: "YOU come back to ME." Ah, no, sorry, I don't have to go back to anyone. You have left me, so it's you who has to earn the right to come back to me, to show me that I can trust you again, not me.

When we love, we think about the other person. You're in love with your ex and you're a slob. What thought do you normally have?

ZERO CONTACT

It's very, very likely that when you cut off all contact, she go crazy. Without knowing it, you have been putting a safety net on her acts; she could come in and go out. She was happy because you were behind like a puppet pleading her. That made her know that by snapping her fingers, she would have you there like a little puppy and that security has made her ignore you and live her life without a single second of anguish over your void, because you haven't disappeared.

When you disappear, she may feel that she no longer has you warming up on the sideline. Perhaps you are going on with your life; perhaps you're inviting someone else to the cinema and giving them expensive little presents. It's then that she might go crazy and call you and if she does so, she's call you or write to you "just to hear from you."

This, little buddy, is just to check that she still has her puppet sitting there and waiting. She only wants you to say that you're sad and in a shitty mess and that you really hope you can arrange to meet up to talk, something pathetically ridiculous. Then at that moment, when she has the net set again, she'll say to you "oh, look... it's better for us not to see each other" or "it's just that you suffocate me" and you're off to be screwed yet again, for being as smart as a piece of scrotum.

If we make zero contact, we have to really do it, right through till the end. If she wants to come back to you, she will tell you openly, she will not disguise it as a "let's meet up to go for a walk or to speak."

• If she wants to know how you are over WhatsApp: don't fucking listen.

• If she wants to meet up to talk: don't fucking listen.

• If you have four missed calls from her at 4:00 in the morning: don't fucking listen.

• If she goes to pick you up from work/university to go for a walk: don't fucking listen.

And when I say "don't fucking listen," it's "don't fucking listen," that is, the WhatsApp remains as read and unanswered (although really, she should already be blocked).

If she writes to you to see if you meet up: it remains as read.

If you wake up and you have four missed calls, you delete them and it's as if AT&T had called you for you to change companies.

If she goes looking for you, you tell her that you can't because you have things to do, that at most perhaps another day. And you leave, with indifference and coldness.

I repeat that if she has thought things through better and wants you to be together and happy again, she will make it clear to you. If she beats around the bush, it means that she only wants to check that her net is still on.

The zero-contact rule can work to recuperate the other person, so that they realize they can't live without you... yes... but that is not the objective, because we can't decide that. But instead, we *can* use the zero-contact rule to recover, something that does depend 100% on ourselves.

That will come or not with time. But the purpose of this book is that you forget her and that you wake up happy, that you go back to being who you used to be, that you believe and trust yourself and that, once you are free from all emotional dependence and from all pain, you decide freely and with a recovered heart who to give it to again. If it's the same person who once trampled on it, well that will be up to you WHEN YOU ARE 100%. Never forget that the priority here is *you*.

The zero-contact rule is 75% of the way to being well. The more strictly you do it, the sooner you will live happily like before, without anguish and with hope, so I hope you have assimilated well how important it is for all of this and that you've decided to carry it out without excuses.

I'm going to leave a piece of advice here of something that can make you screw up, especially breaking the zero-contact rule and also making your suffering multiply:

Drunken nights out are going to take you away from healing. You can be in a shitty state and feel that by having four drinks, you have the confidence in yourself to not give a shit about anything. But it's a false sensation, produced by alcohol toxicity. You will feel a thousand times worse the next day, as the alcohol will depress you during the hangover and you will see everything much blacker, with no way out of this moment that you are going through.

Neither the euphoria when you're drunk as a skunk nor the motherfucker of a hangover in the morning are a reality. Try to get away from both and focus on sport to get that same euphoria naturally.

If I'm telling you this about the drunken nights out, imagine the rest: smoke a joint and the thoughts will torture you at 2000 miles per hour.

Or worse yet, if you do a few lines of coke or meth or acid etc., you will spend days, maybe weeks, having a rotten time.

Being intoxicated/drugged up, we don't perceive things well and we don't think clearly. It's easy for you to screw up, breaking the zero-contact rule. If this happens, you don't know the damage that you'll have done to yourself.

SWEAT, YOU BASTARD

You have to do sport. If you want the short way to get out of all of this, you have to do it. I don't know if you used to do it before and you fancy the idea. But in this case, you have to give it even more of what you have. If you didn't used to do it, you have to start slowly.

The reason (I suppose you'll soak it in better if I explain why, instead of just "because") is that sport makes you feel good and helps us to produce endorphins. When you are distressed, overwhelmed, wanting to cry, it's a gray day, everything reminds you of her, you see everything black etc., put your sneakers and earphones on and go for a run. Listen to music and run. If you've never done it before, you'll do it like an old woman at the start, but it doesn't matter. Run, tire yourself out, don't stop and don't go back home without tiring yourself out, because the psychological pain torturing you with memories will be worse than the suffering of running out of air. Run, at your own pace—if necessary, almost walking—but sweat... tire yourself out; it will help you to arrive home feeling good. Have a shower, eat something and fall straight into bed.

This should be enough for it to be worthwhile and essential to do sport. This could mean running, just as much as it could mean boxing or lifting weights. Do what you want, but exercise your body, look after it, move it... Start taking care of yourself from the outside.

The second positive thing about sport is that it will make you look better. Sign up to the gym and go five days a week—six if you can go Saturday morning—and you will feel fuck-a-doobly amazing. You can now invest that idle time in yourself, in taking care of yourself and in taking care of your diet. Don't be a dickwomble and eat fatty foods or donuts. Let's use this phase in which life is screwing us ever so slightly up the anus to bring out some benefit. Who knows if with a bit of luck while you recover, you get better physically and one day she sees you made into one strapping specimen of the male species, with charisma and self-esteem, and you make her screw herself inside seeing what she lost?

The transformation will be slow and you will need perseverance, but it will be worth it; believe me. Little by little, make an effort, take care of yourself, pamper yourself, eat healthy, buy clothes that look good on you, spend money on a good hairdresser... Dammit, rub little creams all over yourself if necessary. Train with balls. You're improving a lot in your attitude as a man, which will be useful for everything in life, and at the same time you're also improving your physique. You're working on that improved version 2.0 of yourself that you promised me at the beginning, remember?

The third positive point about sport are the new friendships. Everything has now been left behind. Whoever your friends are will continue to be so and will know that they mustn't say even one word about her, either because of common sense or because you have told them not to, since there are some people with fewer lights on in their dimwitted brains than a blow-up refugee boat. These people will come along speaking crap with the objective of gossiping and the only thing they will produce is pain in you when telling you things.

At the gym, in your boxing classes, at your athletics club, on your football team, at rugby... and even if you go to that Zumba thing or Pilates, I don't care. You will meet new people and healthy people too. (People who enjoy themselves doing daytime activities are good people who will bring light to your life; people who live through the night and among addictions will bring you ruin). With healthy people, however, you will go out to Christmas dinner or somewhere else and you will expand your circles little by little.

Sport has to be daily: a routine that makes you have things to do when you finish your obligations, that fills your day and that also gives you that feeling of well-being and good vibes that will make you be someone more attractive and with charisma.

I personally recommend a contact sport; for me, it's worked well. It has taught me a lot in life and it gives you a lot of values that will come in handy in the future.

IT'S ESSENTIAL THAT YOU FULFILL THESE TWO PREMISES: THAT YOU CUT OFF ALL CONTACT AND THAT YOU DO SPORT.

Another point that we could include in this chapter on sport is that of achieving goals. It would be goddamn good as you go along gaining confidence in yourself, feel better and your head has less and less grief as the days go by (obviously, there will be days and days), that you start to propose yourself ambitious goals. Do you want that promotion? Did you want to start your business? Do you have to finish your studies? Show yourself that you can deal with anything, carry out what you have pending and grow. Grow as a person, feel good about yourself, find out how much you are worth and how little you loved yourself when you dragged yourself along for that girl. Let nothing stop you, use the rage in your favor, think about how it will hurt her to look fabulous like you because you're taking care of yourself so much and also finding out that you finally achieved what you always told her you would achieve. There, she will stop feeling pity and will feel admiration and perhaps envy. When you get there, I will have nothing but to congratulate you.

But do it, don't stop doing it and don't think that in another moment it will be better. Every second that you have your head occupied with thinking of productive things, things that will make you grow, it will be one second less of anguish over thinking about her. You will be taking suffering out and you will be putting positivity into your mind.

Remember that in life there are three types of people, nothing more:

- The winners.

- The fighters.

- The losers.

You can choose between the second and the third at any time, but only with time will you arrive at the first. There is no shortcut for this, so try hard and achieve whatever you want. A man of faith has no limit. Use self-love as a cure for it.

Here we are going to talk about the possible doubts or "obstacles" that you might encounter.

As you have seen, the process to feel good is quite simple, at least to explain. Zero contact, sport and, as soon as you have the strength, new goals. That at the same time includes you getting to know new people. You will change your routine and you will get out of your comfort zone etc.

On paper, it's easy; in practice, it's not. Something like this happens with Gandhi's formula to be happy: *Say, think and do the same.* Think about it;

unifying these three things, one is happy in life, but it's not at all easy.

I assure you that if you cut off all contact, do sport and grow spiritually with new goals, knowledge and friendships, you will be happy very soon.

The process will be long, there is no exact cross-multiplication rule whereby for each year of relationship, there are three months of suffering, nor any other nonsense alike. There are people who overcome things earlier and there are people who do so later.

I say that the process will be long because we spend it in a terrible state and, like this, even a week can seem long.

If I speak to you from my experience, what's happened to me is as follows. Day 1: I passed the time in tears; Day 3: I walked alone along the beach and I called a friend telling him how sad I was and how badly I was handling managing things; Day 8: I met new people and told them that it was a bad moment for me; and Day 15: I left the house of a girl I had met two days earlier and went towards the car smiling and thinking "What the fuck? Am I going to be bitter for her?" and I never suffered again for that girl.

What's more, after four months I became infatuated with another girl that I was with for a year and it took me another two years to stop thinking about her… So there is no way to guess exactly what day you will be well. I suppose it's like what happens with yogurts: if it expires on the 13th, at 11:55pm on the 12th you can eat it, but 10 minutes later not anymore? Well the same thing.

Assume it will last whatever it lasts and you're going to be down in the cumdumps, as is only natural.

And since it's something that you are going to have to put up with, make the most of it to make it as bearable as possible. You can spend a month, or a year, suffering in your room, crying and making everything Hell and you may even create a lifelong trauma for yourself.

Or you can cope with it, accepting that you're in a bad way, but that while you get over it you're going to have fun and you can invest your winter into getting as good-looking as possible and meeting up with your friends for all the plans that come up. In summer, you can plan an escape to Ibiza; you decide how to manage your pain. I recommend the second option.

You will have relapses as is normal. We are people, not machines.

You will have moments of loneliness and moments of nostalgia. You will even be surprised when you discover yourself going a few hours without thinking of her at all and the same thing when after a while you relapse again and the desire to break the zero-contact rule returns.

It will be normal for you to die of jealousy or to think absurd things. For example, you might be in bed at 1:00 in the morning on a Saturday night and you're thinking where she might be, if she might have put that dress on that suited her so well and if she might be making out with some guy in that nightclub that she used to like going to.

Well the first thing is to tell you that that thought is normal. The second thing is to tell you that we always remember our exes idealized as having more virtues than they actually have, and even more so when we suffer from emotional dependency. Forget about her; she's not that great.

Second, if she's at a nightclub smooching guys left and right, without thinking about you for a second, while you're a fucking mess in bed, thinking of her, do you think that person is the woman of your life, that she should be the mother of your children and that she deserves to have you going through a tough time because of her?

Imagine for a second that it's not like that, that she decides to leave you because she no longer loves you, in all sincerity, and as such she tells you and it hurts her too. She then goes home and carries on with her calm life, knowing she's hurt you, but that it was inevitable, because she no longer felt what she should have about you. You can't control that and while you're in bed, not able to sleep, she too is at home, trying to distract herself with anything she can to not think about how difficult everything is and wanting you, and then herself, to be okay with each other and be able to be friends someday. Here, I would understand that you feel that you have lost a great woman, although it wouldn't make sense either, because she no longer loves you.

If you have relapses out of missing her, out of jealousy, because of something they've said to you, because of a photo you've seen on Facebook... YOUR FUCKING FAULT FOR NOT HAVING CUT OFF ALL CONTACT. And now, well then, there's only one solution: balls and a cool head. Accept that it's part of the recovery process and turn the page as soon as possible. If you can, go out for a run; if not, distract yourself, call your best friend, tell them what you're going through and afterwards you can speak about something else, something that makes you laugh. It will help you to get your head out of the anguish and reassure it again and to keep fighting.

Perhaps you will see her taking the dog out, or at the supermarket, at the nightclub... and perhaps you will even see her with someone else. Well, accept that since she left you, you haven't gone to a monastery to see if they let you lock yourself in there for life and, as far as can be seen, she hasn't become a nun either, let alone a cloistered nun. This should make you think that she's going about her life and doesn't stop to cry about all of this, which makes the fact that you do even more ridiculous.

Act coldly. If you cross paths and she doesn't see you, don't go and say "hello" or any bullshit like that. You leave.

If she sees you, "hello," smile and goodbye.

If she wants to talk about something, you're in a hurry, you're a very busy person and you tell her that you've arranged to meet with someone and that you're going to arrive late. Even if you're going home and you have nothing to do all day, nothing good can come of stopping to talk to her, nothing that will help you move forward in your recovery.

Accept that she no longer exists, and it's the truth. She's only idealized in your head, but she's not the person you're in love with. She's another person who's similar, but with many more negative things. Don't worry: you'll be able to talk to her again without problems, even go for a walk, but not for now. We need time and to recover, don't screw it up despite seeing yourself at 99%, because you'll relapse and everything you've fought for before will have been of no use.

I promise you that if I see my exes today, I don't care, just like if I see them hand in hand with my best friends: total indifference. But it goes to the extent that I wouldn't care at all if I had a beer with them or not, just like the Chinese lady that I used as an example before.

If, after a reasonable time, a message or a call of hers arrives to see how you are, evaluate how you feel, evaluate what you felt upon seeing it. If there has been 1% of bad vibes, ignore it. If she's waited until now, she can wait a bit more.

You may like to know whether she could be your friend in future, well *I* don't know. You may see her in a completely differently way. As we have said, let's go to what's urgent, which is for you to recover, and then when the moment arrives, we can look at the whole friendship thing.

Either way, in my opinion, being your "friend" as such I don't think is going to happen, or at least one of those of which you only have three of in life. But you *will* be able to have a good relationship, with good vibes and without things from the past that make you fight, nor throwing indirect hints at each other.

In the end the bad things go by and we only have the memory of the good things. Whether you want it or not, it was someone who passed through your life, who contributed things to you and from whom you learned. They probably gave you love in certain moments and you were happy by their side and that will remain as a distant memory. You can arrange to meet up to have lunch, tell each other how things are going, even speak about your current partners, finally without a grudge, and even give each other advice. Yes, don't worry about that, but you have to do things properly like I've told you. If you behave like a stalker, a drag, overwhelming and loony, it will all end terribly and you won't even greet each other for the rest of your lives.

If your heartache makes you always have the last hope of going back to her... Puff... Let's see how I can explain it to you:

Right, in "your state" it's only normal that you want to grab onto a burning nail; the truth is that you may one day get back together again. But I don't think it's a good thing to have that hope. I don't recommend it, because it will make you suffer.

It's better that you continue to have the goal of being happy by yourself, without anyone else. And if, in the future, when you are yourself again and you're up, you talk and you've both missed each other and there are no more grudges and you want to be together again, that's where you decide with a cool head.

What's normal is for you to have learned from all of this and that on your way to your version 2.0, you will meet other girls and you'll know how to identify the things that you don't like, because you associate them with things from other past relationships and cut the crap before having feelings. So you'll be more demanding and selective and will no longer want someone who is a photocopy of your ex, so obviously neither will she. I'm going to give you an example for you to understand it better:

Imagine that your ex is very affectionate, she screws like a fucking goddess, but she doesn't give you the intellectual spark that you need, because she spends the day watching trash TV and she speaks to you about the contestants while you have dinner together, something which you really couldn't care less about, but oh well; "she is how she is and I accept her." In addition, it turns out that her greatest passion is to wear very short skirts and go out and end up drunk every weekend. They tell you that Johnny and Charlie were very close to her or that someone took her home one day. And she says that nothing happened and they don't want anything or that if they want it, she doesn't realize, as they're just friends. And that makes you suffer because you suspect that you've been cheated on more than a high school math exam.

Now imagine that at a pool (now that you'll be stockier than chicken broth if you've listened to me about the sport), you meet a group of girls and there is one that you find especially cool. You talk to her, you laugh and there are good vibes with all of them, but with her more so, so much so that you spend the whole day together, you swap WhatsApp details and in the end you arrange to meet up with her another day to have a glass of wine. You dress yourself up and you vacuum the car etc. You pick her up and take her to a place that you know is going to be fantastic and when you get there, it's the worst night of your life because she's spent the whole dinner talking about Big Brother and Jerry Springer. You've tried to talk to her about other things, but she always carries on all the same, because honestly, she allocates the giving of exactly zero fucks to your life plans or what you did on your last trip.

In addition, she drinks three times as much as you and finally a little bit fed up to your hairy balls you say that you want to go home and she says no and that you should go to some I-don't-know-what kind of nightclub in her neighborhood. You go, feeling obliged, and in the end, she ends up drinking so much that she sucks the water out of the vases, unable to keep herself up.

Do you think that despite this you would keep going and meeting up with her because she has a pretty face, you love her smile and has a bootylicious ass? Or do you think that you'll have put on a prior filter, which you didn't with the other girl and that you'd prefer to say fuckety-bye and carry on with your life, because you know that person isn't right for you?

Well this is the lesson that your ex will leave you and, believe me, you can give it another try with her, but what's normal is that she want something different and once you understand all of this, you must learn and grow.

SEX LIFE AFTER THE BREAKUP

At the beginning, it's only normal that you don't have eyes for other girls; no one will seem pretty enough to you or, in the event that one of them does seem to be, she'll be lacking in something that your ex had better, whether it be her ass, her boobs, that beautiful hair she had or how good she was at Tekken on PlayStation.

You will be blind and even if you were to have the woman of your life before you, you wouldn't see her. It will be as if you were walking with both hands covering up what you have on either side of you. Your feeling and your inner pain make you able to only think of your ex. You will have to heal little by little; let time pass and let that emotional dependence disappear to reopen your eyes and see what is around you.

There is a very clear metaphor that applies very well to this and it's that perhaps, one day, you will realize that you have your hands busy grabbing something that is falling behind and that you refuse to release it. You cling to it with all your strength, without much sense or logic, and all of this despite you yourself knowing that you need to release it to be able to catch what is happening in front of you in the present, which is full of good things.

The most direct and clear piece of advice I can give you here, about your sex life right now or later, is to listen to yourself and only yourself. You should do whatever your body asks you for, you should have the personality to decide if you will go with one girl or another or no girl and not see yourself forced by what your friends or anyone like that will think.

If you one day meet a girl and she's interested in you and you in normal conditions should also be interested in her, but right now it doesn't work out for you or you don't feel like it, don't force yourself. From my own experience, I'll tell you that when you try to substitute, you miss even more. So you might end up in a mess thinking about your ex instead of enjoying the situation.

Giving an example of mine: It has happened to me that, sick and tired of not managing to stop thinking about her, dreaming about her and suffering, I would get drunk. A couple of times that I ended up with some female company, the night was a disaster. Without realizing it, I was looking for my ex in the other girl and everything was strange. It wasn't that girl that I wanted to be with and maybe at that moment my desire to escape made me keep on doing it. But in the end, when the alcohol wore off, when I realized what I was doing, a huge sadness would come over me and a couple of times I stopped, got dressed, apologized and went home alone crying in the car, thinking even more about her.

Because of being a dickwit, because of trying to force things, everything worked out terribly.

To finish with this example, I once met a girl at some friends' wedding; we were talking and we swapped WhatsApp details. We wrote to each other for a few weeks and it just so happened that

I had to pass through her city. It had been a little over a year that things had been over with my ex and with this girl I was starting to fool around again and it was something that I liked, that filled me up, something I hadn't felt in a long time.

I was surprised looking at her responses to my WhatsApps with a smile, to see the playfulness we had, the mischief, to see that she too fancied me etc. There, I began to feel that I was already in the final stretch of my recovery.

Be that as it may, we met up, we slept together and I loved it. The best part was the feeling as I left her house, heading for the bus station.

It was early morning and I was smiling. I felt fan-fucking-tastic; I still remember it. I felt a great inner relief because finally, after more than a year, I had gone to bed with another girl without my ex going through my head and I felt free to love again, losing the fear of going back to missing my ex in bed.

With that girl I felt like it. I liked her and I did things calmly, in a planned manner and out of attraction... And it turned out well. Meeting this same girl four months earlier in a bar at 3:00 in the morning, and in the rush of wanting to forget, would definitely have been another failure.

So be patient, don't force yourself to get into the good-looking girls you see, to see if something happens and if you get better. Don't get involved sexually with old friends you had a flirtationship with, just because you think that "you get a nail out by nailing," because you may well look desperate. That can be smelt and you lose the friend. If you like her, try it when you feel good.

If you are going to review old hook-ups, things that you left halfway etc., write or call the girl you *really* liked, go out and have fun and if the occasion comes up and you feel like it, sleep with one or a thousand, but don't look for the cure to your upset in quick sex with whoever. Also, going hardcore will scare the girl, even if she likes you. It usually creates the opposite reaction and you can go home being rejected by more than you can count and with your ex in the head, which will be worse than a kick in the balls.

Slowly—there is no exact date—let everything happen and everything come. And believe me, you will have fun with a woman again, even more than with your ex.

DOES LOVE SICKNESS HAPPEN MORE THAN ONCE OR IS IT LIKE CHICKENPOX?

From my experience I would say yes, it does happen more than once, but with nuances.

The first love destroys you, you don't know where it comes from, you don't understand anything and it's such a beautiful, vivid feeling and that you haven't had before, that you brim over with it and you don't know how to face it.

If it happens to you a second time, you will identify the things that happened to you in the first and you will suffer the same, but already knowing that you are not going to die, just like you didn't the other time, although at times you thought you were about to do so. You will see that you have the same thoughts and you will use what you learned in the previous heartache to manage it better this time, even though the second love may be stronger than the first and even hurt your soul.

If it happens to you a third time and you see that the processes are repeated again, you will have learned to have the control over yourself to get out of the grief and be well again, despite understanding that you love the other person and that it's normal for you to feel that way. But you have to get cured like you did other times, so it's there that you use all those feelings and write a book like this one.

So lose your fear of what will happen in the future and live in the present, be as happy as you can without thinking that this suffering will return to you again in a few years' time. Nobody can know that.

What I can assure you is that, if you have a breakup in the future, you will know how to handle it better.

WILL I EVER COMPLETELY FORGET OR WILL I ALWAYS KEEP REMEMBERING MY EX AND COMPARING HER?

As my favorite singer (Canserbero, Caracas) says: "I know there are beautiful memories, but it's not wise to have memories because of obsession."

The memories are no longer going to be of any use. They can't help you and there is no way to go back in time and experience the good things again. It won't help you to beat yourself up remembering that day that you forgot to go and pick her up and how she got very angry and thinking that perhaps from that day everything started go downhill.

Even less should you remember how you were a moron for not realizing that that guy who was supposedly her friend in the end was something more than that.

Don't beat yourself up over things that have already gone by and start to forget it. That was your other "me" and you should no longer worry about anything that happened. Now is the time to learn to live in the present, to force things so that you have a present like you deserve and, therefore, your past from today onwards will be damn brilliant because you're building a Hell of a present. The future, which doesn't exist, will be great the day it arrives, because it will come as a present and you will you have made sure it's good.

Learn to have positive thoughts: Imagine that your soccer team goes to the Mercedes-Benz Stadium to play for the MLS Cup and they leave losing 6-0. Do you think the way to deal with that is to get everyone together in training to continually remember the thrashing they were given and how useless they are? Maybe continually blame themselves? Maybe give up and never participate in any MLS Cup ever again?

What's normal is for them to leave feeling throttled and rabid and that they try three time as hard to train waiting for the next game against Atlanta United FC to get them or die trying. They will prepare to be better, without forgetting what has happened, but without beating themselves up over it. They simply see where they have failed, to do better in future when they have the opportunity.

You must do the same. Don't beat yourself up. Forget it. Nothing matters anymore and you are never, ever going to achieve anything by remembering the past. It doesn't matter what it is; there will never be even the most insignificant change in your life on the basis of remembering the past. And in the meantime you get upset, you go over and over things in your head, you cry, you become frustrated, you feel that pain time and time again, remembering as if you were living it again. While you do that, you are taking time out of thinking about how to improve your present.

I want you to know that it's only normal for you to have those thoughts and that obsession in your memories. It's only normal in the entire process and something that happens to all of us. Knowing how to control it, knowing how to distract yourself when they come at you, knowing how to focus your thoughts on something productive or simply happy, will make those thoughts less and less frequent every day. It's like someone who is trying to quit smoking and who, every time they're dying to light a cigarette, ignores it, starts doing something else and carries on with their life. Every time your willpower makes you overcome it, you will be giving a blow to your discomfort and to your agony and you will be killing it just that little more.

Fight and wrestle. You are here for that: to fight against those memories and to overcome everything based on courage and balls, which is what will make you, instead of being a sad guy anchored in his past, be a proud man, with your head held high, who conquers life like a boss.

These shitty feelings that you have right now, well focused can be amazing: normally the human being needs motivation to do things. They may invite you to a birthday party and you don't at all feel like going, but they tell you that I-don't-know-who is going and you are fucking dying to be the first there.

You need the motivation of money to get up at 7:00 in the morning and go to that job that you don't like for shit. The salary motivates you to pay the bills, like the vast majority of people and like the donkey that goes along chasing his carrot.

Normally the human being can't care less and is lazy, it settles with what it has and doesn't like making more of an effort than that necessary. That's why there are more people with bellies than with abs.

Now what's most likely is that you have an enormous inner rage and desire for revenge towards your ex. But it's not violent revenge, but rather you would love her to one day regret all of this and not be with you and suffer for not having you, as you are now. It's a normal feeling to pay back the pain by instinct.

Okay, perfect, use this to your advantage. Instead of getting frustrated because she's not with you, make it hurt her in the future:

Get handsome. It's time for the gym, for a diet, to go for a run, for the Sun to kiss you and to be tanned. Can you imagine yourself with that convertible that you have always liked, with your arms, your haircut as if you were that Beckham guy and your you-can't-touch-this "beach babe" clothes? Imagine getting out of the car while you smile at your ex in a good mood, because you have already overcome things and you'll see how they all say to her "whoahhh, is that your *ex*?" while they drool and your girlfriend in a bad way, because of the strapping guy you've now become. Well, GET TO IT.

Can you imagine finishing your studies with a high mark, finding that amazing job in Miami that pays you a fortune and spending the day travelling? Think about how it would be to come on vacation to your city and for her to see that you have triumphed in life, look sideways at the boy she's with now, compare you both and regret it. GET TO IT.

And all the times you'd told her that you wanted to start your own business? Well, imagine that you start it up and thanks to your hard work, it goes freaking amazingly. After a while, you meet up with her and you go to have lunch in an awesome place, you tell her how well your business is going and you get your wallet out and pay. She realizes that you now have enough dough to bury her in bank bills. GET TO IT.

Use that grudge and that bad mood as motivation to achieve your goals. Move forward with it.

If I tell you the truth, when you have achieved any of the things that you have set yourself out of anger, you're not going to give more than zero flying fucks about her and you're not even going to have time to go and have anything with her, nor will it interest you to, as strange as it may sound now. But all that benefit that you've created using that motivation will remain in you forever. And well, if I'm wrong and if you do still want to talk to her in a bar, well great for you. Use some false modesty and give yourself the guilty pleasure of leaving her screwed.

A digression I want to make in this chapter is that everything happens for a reason; everything is perfect.

It's a great truth that, when we look back on life, everything has a meaning and everything fits perfectly into the history of your life. That fight made you change your friends and thanks to that, you made a new group that has helped you professionally or thanks to the fact that the car was left stranded at that gas station, you met a person who was later extremely important in your life. If you even think about it, something happened for you to meet your ex and it was strictly necessary.

Well, following this rule of logic, what is happening to you should be necessary for something good that awaits you in the future. Don't you think so?

On the other hand, taking revenge on your ex is showing her that you still love her, and you will be giving her the victory over you.

Be a polite man, with honor, with manhood and with manners. Be a gentleman and withdraw without further ado, don't waste your time in cursing her with friends, nor in speaking ill of her to acquaintances. Just be indifferent, as if you were above all of this, and it will make you be just that.

Don't act like a resentful, spoilt little boy and do it like a man from head to toe. You will appreciate it when everything has gone by and it will help you to know how to act in future, seeing all the good that it has brought you.

Also, you honestly can't be goddamn bothered wasting time in life, which is precious, on hating someone. Use your time for nice things like loving yourself, as we have spoken about before. There is also a universal and proven truth that goes "the more love you give, the better you feel and the more hatred you keep, the worse." So do it for yourself. Don't hold resentment inside that will cause sickness; it will sour your character and you will also be uglier.

AND WHAT IS SHE FEELING? WILL I
ALWAYS FEEL THE SAME WAY ABOUT MY
EX?

Firstly, if what you are wondering is if you can fall in love again: No, definitely not... Keep in mind that there are eight billion people in the world, of which let's say half—four billion—are in your range of sexual tastes if it's that you are heterosexual or homosexual and not bisexual. And you think that the only person on the whole planet with whom you will be happy and fall in love with is one who lives four streets away and who doesn't even want to be with you? What bullshit, pal. It's ridiculous no matter *how* you look at it.

About what she feels, supposedly in general women and men can suffer in the same way.

We are going to put ourselves in the situation where *she's* the one who leaves *you* and we are going to put ourselves in the improbable case that for some strange reason she's going to be locked up at home for five years without leaving a single second, just studying and without a cell phone.

Surely that security that it would give you to know that no one else will touch her, nor will she fall in love or anything like that, would make you feel less fucked up and calmer than you are right now.

Well, whoever dumps someone has a similar feeling of tranquility. I don't think she despairs thinking about you, but there will always be small moments in which she thinks of you and that make her nostalgic.

But either way, she'll get over it quickly, which is just one more reason for you to not waste time thinking about someone who doesn't love you.

I quote from something Queco said in 2008:

Women rebuild their lives and, from time to time, when they have doubts if their new mister is what they were looking for, they feel a jab: Is he there? Does he have another girl? And then they send a pathetic SMS/WhatsApp like "I hope you're well." One of these can screw with you for three or four days if you do things properly, and a month if you reply. Before this, indifference. It doesn't mean anything. It's the way they have of putting you warming up on the sideline and raising their self-esteem on the way.

About the question of whether you will always love her the same as now, the answer is a big, fat, Greek NO. What's normal is that you suffer for her for a period of time, you miss her and you want to get back with her. Also, you will only remember the good things, as if nothing bad had happened in all that time. Then as a second step towards oblivion, you will move on to hating her and you won't even be able to see her. You will wish her the worst, with as much damage as she did to you, and you will hold a grudge against her. You will remember her in a shit-stained light.

And finally, you will move on to indifference. You will appreciate the good moments, you will count things that you did without any kind of hatred or internal love and you will see it as part of a past that you no longer care about. You will even be able to go have something to drink outside a bar while she's right next to you with her new partner and you won't care at all about them, as if they were strangers.

There is a fairly recurring conduct in human behavior: testing. I'm going to explain below what this word means:

The person who is dumped in a breakup will periodically receive "evidence" from the r ex to find out if they "are still there." This means that while you are depressed, feeling a huge void not able to be filled by anything and believing that no one will *ever* be able to fill it because she was unique, she has already cut off all communication with you. However, *she* doesn't feel such a void, because in her subconscious she knows that you are there, that you haven't forgotten her and that perhaps if it goes wrong, she can talk to you and that you get back together. That gives her peace of mind and makes her brain not make her distress with your memory, as is happening to you.

But what she will do when she doesn't hear from you for a while, to replace that "safety net" and calm down again when she gets bored in her new and passionate life, will be to contact you for any stupid little thing, such as, for example, a "hey, I wanted to know how are you" or a "I'm sending you a photo to see which dress you like the most for my cousin's wedding"—whatever, anything ridiculous—and she honestly doesn't care about your answer. If she cared in the slightest about you, she wouldn't have left you suffering while she went on with her new life.

The only thing she expects from you is a "I'm in a bad way… But oh well…" or "you're very pretty in the red dress; tell me you won't hook up with anyone" or things like that. Even if she doesn't achieve those phrases directly, she might force them out to achieve them like "Johnny's coming to the wedding hahaha, but I'll ignore him" to awaken your jealousy and get what she wants.

She may even come to give you hope as long as seeing if, as my father says, "when they go 'pss', you wag your tail" (referring to dogs I suppose) with phrases like "Hey, how about we arrange to meet up someday to have a drink of something and speak properly?": something which will never happen, by the way. Once she has her net set again, knowing that you're warming up on the sideline, ready to come out, she will disappear until she needs another boost of self-esteem.

It's not that this behavior is something unique to your ex and that she's more evil than the rest, but rather that it's something generalized in human behavior and that we do almost instinctively. I myself recognize that I've done it in my earlier relationships many years ago and it's something that I wouldn't do today, nor do I do, nor will I do.

Very well then, we've already talked about the zero-contact rule, how bad it is for our recovery to have news of her and why we had to cut off all communication, but we can't go and live in

Antarctica either. If she wants to, she will know how to communicate: from calling directly from her cell phone or someone else's with some sort of an excuse, to calling someone who is with you and telling them to pass the phone or anything you can think of.

On how to act before the testing, I can give you several pieces of advice and also teach you a rule: The five-second rule.

Before any type of testing, we are busy. I'll explain:

If we're sprawled in bed crying and our cell phone rings, we wait five seconds and then pick up as normal:

- Hello?

- Hi Louis.

- Hi Louisa.

- I thought of you and I'm just calling to see how you are.

- Emmm okay… Cool… (nonchalantly) but it's not a great moment right now. Let me call you in ten minutes' time.

- Okay! Speak in a bit then.

- Speak soon.

Right, that has to be the call. With ten seconds, it's more than enough. Anything that drags on after this is screwing you over and doing you harm. Perhaps you don't even believe it right now, but if you don't follow exactly what I say and believe yourself to be smarter than anyone else, you will end up realizing it by yourself.

Before continuing, I am going to clarify a question that you probably have in your head: What if it turns out that she's calling me to tell me that she's thought things through properly, that I'm the man of her life and that she wants to be with me and wants for us to never separate again?

Okay, well in that case, she calls you and tells you that. She doesn't call you to see how you are and since, only by coincidence, you're already speaking, say: "well, you know what, I've just remembered that you're the man of my life." No, it doesn't go like that.

If she wants to come and get back with you, full of regret, she will find the way to go to your house and ask for your forgiveness and beg you for another chance, even if you've moved house, city and country, as *you* would have done if it depended on that to get back with her again.

Someone who wants to be with another person tells them directly. If this doesn't happen, it's because they don't want to be with you, so go back to the point where I told you to love yourself and to have honor, dignity and self-love. Don't be silly at the other end of the phone, telling her what she wants to hear, when she's been ignoring you for some time now, happy with her new life.

Let's keep going. After that conversation, you hang up the phone and don't call again, ever, under any circumstances.

For two main reasons:

- You've been waiting for God-knows-how-long for that call that would never come; how many times have you heard it vibrating and have you taken your phone out in half a second to see if it was her, and when you saw that you didn't even have a WhatsApp from her, or a call, or anything, have you felt disappointed? How many times have you left your cell phone in your room to not have the continuous idea of calling her or looking at the screen and have you wished when you got home to have something from her? Or even your stomach has shrunk when you saw that you had several WhatsApps and when looking at them, not one was from her. Well now it's your turn, now we're going to turn the story around and it's going to be her who's going to be looking at her phone to see why you don't call, calling herself from the home phone to see if she has coverage. Now *you* have the power. Fuck her.

- We are going to show ourselves self-love and respect. You will feel better taking this small step, where you don't put yourself below her ever again and you're like a little lapdog, but rather in this situation it's now *her* who calls *you* and *you* who is so busy that you can't answer and you also have such an incredible life that you forget about calling her afterwards.

If you follow this to the letter, she's going to go into panic mode, because you will be taking her net off her. She no longer has you on the other side like an idiot; she no longer has anyone wrapped around her little finger. She will probably insist on calling; don't be impatient, don't be stupid and spoil it now. Don't answer. There is nothing in that call that can do you any good, believe me, absolutely nothing.

If she wants to get back with you, she will come to your house to say it to your face, because she'll understand that you're upset and that she now has to work for it. And let us be clear, do you think that if she had the intention of saying to you "I love you a lot, I want to get back with you, forgive me, my love," handing her heart in to you, she would be going to change her mind thinking "Ah,

he isn't taking it… Well I don't love him anymore."
No, right?

Because if you think so, *you* use that same logic, call her on Saturday night when she's out with her friends dancing reggaeton and if she doesn't take it, you decide that you no longer love her and you'll have overcome all of this in record time.

Let the phone ring and only in the event that it should be somewhat annoying, pick up when five seconds have gone by. And don't drag the conversation on for longer than ten seconds, for your own good. Your state now that you're still in the process of recuperating your self-esteem may make you hesitate and you may think that "she's different" and that she perhaps wants to talk to fix things. Very well then, when you're wrong and suffer, remember what you did wrong and start from the beginning again.

The following test-call should look something like this:

- Hello?

- Louis…? Fuck, I've called you twenty times and you haven't called me back (in a shitty mood).

- Yes… It's just that I'm constantly on the go and it was too late when I came home to call you. You've just caught me going into the cinema/the soccer/class/work/my cult. I'll call you when I'm done, really.

- But it's just a moment.

- No, but I really can't. I'll call you. Goodbye.

YOU HANG UP AND DON'T CALL.

We're going to send her the message that you are not to be played around with, that you are a man in conditions who sees things very clearly and that you don't have time for little girly things. You will have put yourself above her and you will have picked up your pride off the floor, you will have cleaned it off and you will have put it back where it always should have been.

Here to end this, I would like to quote a text written by Vedma in 2015 and of which I haven't edited one single comma, because touching something would be to make it worse:

Look, when it's you who dumps, various phases are gone through: euphoria for having done the right thing, new life, etc. The months go by and that euphoria disappears, nothing is new, you get a little bit bored, the queue of admirers like the entrance to see Justin Bieber that you thought you had isn't such and it looks more like the queue of a supermarket at 4:00pm on a Monday. Life outside the couple isn't as pretty as you thought and you wonder if you made the right choice. The doubt comes. And you think, do they still love me? If I look for them, will I find them? And you try... testing. If they answer, take that, I'm fucking amazing, they still love me, I can have whoever I want because look at how wonderful I am. If they don't answer... Fuck, do they no longer love me? Did they care that little about me? It can't be; they loved me so much. They can't have received it... Testing 2 with a slight grudge.

If you answer to the second take, you'll see... they still love me. I wonder what the number is of the hottie from the gym? I might send him a dirty photo to see if we can fuck...

If you don't answer... extreme rage, they don't love me, what a wasted life, I thought they loved me more... And they experience the same grief that *you* went through when they left you. In the end it's selfishness. Me, me, me and whoever comes afterwards, fuck them.

Wipe-out and new account. Don't drag your fears or prejudices along from your past relationships. Every person is a world of their own and you have to love again without fear of being betrayed and without fear of pain. Even if they have cheated on you and you have suffered the insufferable, it doesn't matter.

Never suffer in advance, don't be someone who's jealous and who thinks that she will meet someone and leave you like the other one did. You will never find two identical women and you have to trust blindly and give all the freedom and trust to the person you love, as it will be the nicest present you can give them.

Also, out of curiosities of human behavior, when you are jealous and restrictive with her, you generate the opposite effect. If you prohibit her from going out with her friends, she will feel the desire to do what is forbidden and she will want to do it when it's something that perhaps she had never thought of before. If you get jealous and become a drag with one of her friends and you start bombarding her with questions about him or mistrust, you're going to make her end up noticing him.

Don't blame your new partner for the mistakes of the old one. It will only bring you problems and you will relive bad moments from the past.

As an example, I want to give you one that surprised me back then:

I have a friend who in general couldn't care less about things. He is someone who has the concept internalized by nature of not thinking if they are cheating on him of if they let him cheat. He doesn't dedicate a thousandth of a second to that thought and is therefore intelligent, because he never, ever suffers in advance. If the day comes in which he sees that she has been with someone else, he simply dumps her and that's it, without getting hot-headed beforehand.

Right, this friend of mine had had his girlfriend for years already and I remember myself once being in the house where they lived. She started to tell how she was going to go off with four single (female) friends to Punta Cana, which for any man could mean entering in panic and a clear indication that they have to forbid it or start to sharpening those claws in order to be ready the beauty cheated on her beast. But in my friend's case, it was like someone who hears rain; the conversation went something like this:

- Girlfriend: Next week, I'm going to Punta Cana for nine days "with some girlfriends."

- Friend: Okay, have a great time.

- G: … Ermmm…

- F: What?

- G: Don't you care?

- F: No… I'm happy for you.

- G: Do you not love me or what? Do you not care if I go to Punta Cana "with my girlfriends"? Do you know what people go to Punta Cana for?

- F: No, dammit… I don't know… What do you want? Do whatever you want. I trust you.

- G: It actually seems like you can't give a fuck.

- F: No… But I just don't know what you want me to say.

Well, the conversation must have flipped your mind and anyone who's ever had a girlfriend knows that these conversations with women are real and they themselves admit it laughing. The fact is that she didn't go anywhere because she thought: "This bastard wants me to go… Let's see if it's that he wants to stay here alone to fuck another girl." So in short, by not giving it importance and without showing jealousy, he saved himself a situation he wouldn't have given a shit about, but that would have bothered a lot of men and I don't think that they would have been able to continue a normal relationship afterwards.

And what is very clear to me is that, if he had said that if she were to go on that trip then the relationship would be over, in a bad mood, she would have gone, and on top of that she would have done so angry with him, because "it's just that he suffocates me and he doesn't let me live my life" and they may very well have prescribed a good claw-sharpening to my pal.

Another example that I always liked and although it may sound ugly, I hope nobody takes it that way. I'd like to explain it, because I think it perfectly defines human behavior. It's that of taking the dog out for a walk as a simile of life as a couple:

If I take my dog out to go for a walk and I'm on to him every two seconds saying: "hey, don't touch that," "hey, don't eat that," "heyyy pssss heyyy come," "hey don't go," "heyy" etc., the dog is going to care less and less about me, because he knows that I'm behind him. He's going to do whatever he wants, with me behind him like a stupid fucktrumpet trying to stop him all the time.

If, instead of that, I take the dog out and I ignore him and keep to myself, the dog doesn't separate itself from my side and is aware of my every move and tries to not go too far; he wouldn't want to lose me out of sight and be left out alone on the street all night.

Well something like this happens to humans, to all of them without exception. So learn this and give all the freedom in the world to your new partner and don't suffer in advance. Let them do and undo, enter and leave, and that freedom will make them love you even more, and if they love you, they will be at your side as an absolute priority in life.

As Canserbero very well said: The secret of life to enjoy every moment is that you must sing as if no one were listening to you, you must dance as if no one were watching you and you must love without fear of being betrayed, although obviously without giving priority to whoever has not given priority to you.

And about your behavior, you have to learn how much you've suffered with their lies, if there have been any, so that you don't lie to someone *you* love.

Take in all the pain that lies and deceit can cause in someone who loves you blindly and who puts all their trust in you. Now that you know, be someone who is good, be a "mensch" as the Jews say and have a good heart. Don't betray whoever your next partner is in this life and act like a real man always looking her in the eyes to say the truth.

If there were no lies in your breakup, if everything was healthy and the love simply ran out, but even so you feel like shite, learn how much a breakup can hurt, how much every word means and the care that you have to take with the other person.

If you have a second breakup and it's you the one who dumps, you know how much damage testing does, so don't do it to her to raise your self-esteem.

Love your new partner and love her with all your heart, make her the happiest woman in the world, take advantage of everything you've learned in your relationship or past relationships to polish those little things, to know how to treat her even better and be happy again being in love without fear of things going wrong.

Little by little.

You have to know that you will not see results and happiness the first day. You will probably feel euphoria as you read the book and will be super motivated when you finish it, but the pain will still be there. You have to go through a necessary mourning for having loved someone and you have to accept it as something natural, even be thankful for it, because all this feeling of grief comes as a hangover of such beauty as you have felt in the past and as the song goes "sufre más el que no ama" (he who does not love suffers the most).

You will have a path full of falls and you will have to get up. You will have low moments, a bad hangover, times when you hear of her, times when you do something that reminds you of her, a smell... Anything can hit you and you will fall. Then you will have to get up, open your trousers, look down, see your balls, remember who you are and how much you are worth and go back to the fight.

And when you're back and you are feeling strong, when you see that there are moments longer than you can imagine in which your brain rests from her and thinks about other things and when you see that you are getting out of this, another stumble will come along and you will have to get up again .

All of this will continue as so until the day comes when the falls are already small stumbles, your eyes begin to see other girls and your memories are no longer so traumatic, nor will you think about her being with another. You will become bitter, you will simply have neutral memories, you will keep the good in your head and you will wish her the best, without your life going too far into knowing how she might be.

But anyway, accept that you have to go through a sentimental mourning for that loved person and that the road will have ups and downs. Remember also that if this were not to happen like this, you should be worried because by the looks of things, you are a sociopath without the normal feelings of a human being, and what is worse, an idiot who has spent a few euros on a book he doesn't need, instead of using them on a lottery ticket, to see if you get lucky.

Regarding your friends, let me tell you something: yes, they were right, even if it hurts to admit it.

Yes, buddy, this is how it is and it's 100% of the times.

If your group of friends/family/people close to you tell you that she's mean and she bosses you around, the fact is that she does. If they tell you that she's with someone else, the fact is that she is. If they tell you that she's bitter, and since you've been with her, you are just as bitter as she is, the fact is that she is, and so are you. And so on and so on.

Your friends have nothing to gain by telling you the truths to your face, while they do have a lot to lose because of meddling with things in your life and that of your partner. So appreciate whoever shows you that they care for you, that they worry and that they want what's best for you, getting themselves into a mess that they could avoid, just because of your friendship.

You can headbutt yourself with the same thing eternally, you can think that everyone is wrong, that you are smarter and that they have it in for her just "because" and you can argue with everyone because you're so confused that you don't know how to act. But you should know that they are right.

So when you want to cling to whatever to try to convince yourself that your friends are wrong and that she's the best, always try to be polite with them, be calm, be understanding and maintain your pose, so that the day you have to say "sorry, I was wrong; I didn't see that you were saying it for my own good and you were right," they still want to listen to you.

I know quite a few morons who ended only because of their arrogance and bad manners, ending up shouting and insulting everyone, when their friends were speaking to them with all the sincerity and love in the world to help them.

So now you know that to clear things up for yourself, where you see smoke there is fire. It might just be that if your friends tell you that you're going the wrong way, the fact is that you really are going the wrong way.

OKAY, VERY NICE, BUT NOW HOW DO I START?

I think if the book ended without this part you would be left halfway thinking, "What? Now he's leaving me alone? You must be kidding!"

Well as Mufasa said in The Lion King: "I have already shown you the way; now you will have to travel it alone." So get on with it. You know that you have to put your balls before your weakness and that you have to be intelligent. Always be intelligent! Apart from that, you know that you have to fill your time with sport and leisure activities, that you have to build something in life and that you have to renew yourself, in addition to not hearing at all from her, either directly or indirectly.

Here, too, everything is already invented. You could think that this Romojaro guy doesn't have a piss-flapping clue and that it's going to do you some real good to stalk her Facebook page every morning, because you know her password and that you will heal more quickly, but you will be screwing with her. I'm telling you now.

Start now and don't despair in relapses, have faith, keep going ahead, fight, renew yourself and evolve, be more of a man, be more charismatic and have more light.

When you need it, if your will falters, if you have a bad day, re-read, feel identified again with what I wrote back then, gain strength again and keep going ahead as you get out of this.

If you screw up, it doesn't matter. Get up, shake off the dust and go back to the fight.

Is there any one of you reading this book who is going to give up? Is anyone going to stay on the side of the road crying? No, right? Well you know it: we will get out thanks to our balls.

Start getting out of this today, don't wait for tomorrow and don't waste any more time.

Now that you have done everything necessary step by step to get rid of the anguish and sadness, release the last burden.

You have to forgive all the damage she did to you, you have to forgive her and not carry hatred or a grudge on the inside. You have to do it for yourself, to free yourself, to live more and better.

Forgive every last detail and if you see her again, speak to her properly, without bad words and without bad gestures.

Forgiveness is necessary at the end of the whole process, because for as long as you keep holding on to feelings (good or bad) you will never have completely overcome it. You need to do it for yourself; you will never have so much self-esteem and light of your own as when you release yourself from all the burdens on your heart.

You have to do it for yourself, but you also have to understand that she, like you, is human and that she could have been wrong. She could have been wrong a thousand times and in the future, when she remembers the damage she did to you, she will probably regret it, so forgive her. Wish her the best from your heart and reconsider for a moment, the person so different, wise and mature that you are now, after the past experience.

And here ends this manual of life and optimism. I hope to have given you enough strength to triumph over everything, that you have internalized everything that has been said and that you write to me very soon to tell me that you feel good and that you wake up happy again.

www.ingramcontent.com/pod-product-compliance
Lightning Source LLC
Chambersburg PA
CBHW071225240726
48654CB00009B/931